The Bronze Butterfly

From Small Beginnings to
World Events All Under a
Fierce Media Spotlight

David S. Smith

authorHOUSE®

AuthorHouse™ UK
1663 Liberty Drive
Bloomington, IN 47403 USA
www.authorhouse.co.uk
Phone: 0800.197.4150

Published by AuthorHouse 08/24/2018

ISBN: 978-1-5462-9698-0 (sc)
ISBN: 978-1-5462-9699-7 (e)

Print information available on the last page.

Preface

The story, set five years into the future brings together a series of situations and advances in broadcast technology that through news coverage worldwide sets out to shape and influence world affairs.

At the same time using both humour and keen observation it confronts serious moral issues.

David S. Smith 2018

My wife Gay patiently read my manuscript correcting my lapses for which I am eternally grateful.

Previous books by this author, Lily (Authorhouse 2014) the story of his mother's life from her birth in Birmingham covering a period from 1911 to the end of the Second World War.

The Stonnall Brigade(Authorhouse 2015) is a collection of 60 short stories.

Contents

1. The Third Eye 1
2. Waking and sleeping 6
3. Radley Airfield 21
4. Down at the Stock Exchange 30
5. Butterfly World 33
6. The Last Ferry 40
7. The First Landing...........................45
8. A Town at War 57
9. First Confrontation 66
10. The Challenge 72
11. World Reaction 77
12. European Union 81
13. The United Nations........................84
14. Realisation.....................................90

Chapter 1
The Third Eye

It was a quiet day in the news hall. Network head Joe Dyke paced the floor, news was money and as the massive wall monitors that tracked the world-wide rating points for station affiliates fell lower and lower Joe prayed for a world disaster. As he walked around the vast news hall he could see the world from desk to desk Tokyo to New York, Sydney to Caracas. The world got its news through London.

Joe had run a small London based freelance news agency, he had come through the school of hard knocks and worked for the toughest news editors from regional newspapers through to Fleet Street. He had seen the decline in the printed word and moved to television news.

Joe, like all good newspaper men was a bastard, he had no scruples just an unquenchable thirst for a story.

If his mother had been caught in bed with a six-foot six gypsy his questions would be, "did you get it on film, are you sure he wasn't seven feet and did you get a quote?" He was an uncompromising bastard, in fact he gave bastards a bad name and in a world that craved for news he was king. He had that great ability to find a story that would shake a nation where anyone else would have dismissed it to a down the page one liner.

Like many newsmen he modelled his early years on the Hollywood B movie image of the investigative reporter working against all the odds to deliver the three-deck headline and the great by-line.

One disaster is another person's opportunity and the climax in 2010 of the world recession gave Joe Dyke just that. The cost of maintaining its world news service was the first big blow to the BBC and the cost saving that brought about the night of the long knives saw an end to the World News Network as we knew it.

The same fate also hit the other entire world news providers from CNN to Reuters, the time had come for a new way of thinking.

Like all disasters something rises from the ashes and again the combination of new technology, entrepreneurship, guts and imagination gave Joe Dyke that drive to capitalise on others' misfortune that came to make London the centre of world news, created the fastest growing company on any Stock Exchange and made Joe Dyke a multi-billionaire in five years.

Joe bought the rights to a micro camera sound system that had instant satellite connectivity, he then set about franchising the system to the world's newshounds, selling rights to station affiliates who were all hungry for news and fed it to and distributed it through the London control centre, and the rest is history.

"Third Eye News" the window on the world was founded and almost overnight filled the gap made by declining funding for news services. Computers replaced overheads that had crippled the networks, newshounds were paid the minute their contribution was screened based on the transmitting stations' rating point at that moment and this included all repeat fees. Stations developed the multi screen technology that satisfied the demand for the insatiable call for news. A Third Eye newshound is a hunter, a ruthless hungry wolf that sometimes hunts alone sometimes in pairs and often in packs, his role is to track down stories and ring every ounce out of them and move to the next prey.

Computers also link stories so apparently unrelated areas come together instantly linking by word, area, business or activity, things that many people would like to keep under the bed rather than on top of it.

Five years of success had not blunted Joe Dyke's nose for news and despite his achievements his home was the news hall, he rarely went out further than the roof top garden that surrounded his penthouse flat, was past regular sex, had few friends and lived on takeaways. He saw this as his own security, if no one got near him no one knew him.

He had long ago left a wife and two children behind in Wolverhampton and a trust fund kept them in a modest way, he chose not to contact them and they returned the compliment.

Chapter 2
Waking and sleeping

As one part of the universe woke up to a dull January morning another part basked in the sunshine of a summer's evening burning good meat on their barbeques, while the remainder went about their morning or afternoon business. Hopefully at some point they will all find time to make the news or watch television and push up the rating points.

As the news hall began to buzz but in a dull way that highlighted a slow news day Joe reflected on how a population of billions could fail to produce a decent juicy story. He went on line to scan the international papers but all they had were stories Third Eye News had already run.

The news desk editors hated Joe looking over their shoulders peering at the reports coming in from the newshounds, they always felt that he would spot a story they had missed.

"Stop!" snarled Joe "what's that?" "Oh nothing, just a local story from Birmingham Airport". The mention of Birmingham made his hackles rise, something deep in his Wolverhampton background always made him flinch at the sound of this hated city. His early years as a reporter on the Express and Star evening newspaper had been driven by a news editor paranoid about beating the Birmingham Evening Mail to every story. "Who's covering this story?" barked Joe. "Jackie and Phil", came the editor's response. Jackie and Phil were a team, they worked together to get every angle on a story, what Phil missed Jackie caught and what Jackie missed Phil caught, they were the perfect newshound team they saw news as both words and pictures in the way the reporter and cameraman teams had in the old days.

"Patch me through to a link and let me follow the story on my monitor". Joe was warming to the chase.

Jackie and Phil were an odd pair, Phil had been a probation officer and deep down admired many of his clients on the basis that they had more excitement in their lives than he did. He spent hours in the Magistrates Court listening to case after case and then having to interview offenders and produce reports, many were just sad cases but occasionally there were the juicy stories that he wished he could have followed and felt some of their excitement.

Jackie had been a benefits clerk working for the local council but at night she changed into a Karaoke diva, there wasn't a star that she couldn't impersonate.

They met in a bar, two unfulfilled lost souls looking for a role and becoming newshounds gave them that magical spur to a new life together.

Not that they lived together but rather more shared lives. They could have moments of passion, part and return as if neither had gone away, but they did have that great understanding of each other that made them so good as a team.

Amongst the thousand odd worldwide newshound teams Joe had his favourites and although he would never let them know Jackie and Phil were amongst the best and amongst the top earners. News desk editors would feed top stories to them knowing they would deliver a top job, in turn they were amongst the top earners each making £250,000 on a good year.

Jackie was interviewing a group of elderly men and women who all looked fit and well with a mass of white flat caps and blue rinse hair with Velcro tab shoes that saved on laces and buckles.

They were standing outside Birmingham Airport complete with cases and golf bags and looking ready for a fight in the way only true wrinklies can.

They were a group of friends that travelled each year from their homes in Wednesfield to fly for their cheap six week break on the Mediterranean holiday island of Menorca. Every year it was six weeks holiday at San Cristobal golf resort with days of golf and nights of card games.

An extremely agitated man in a check shirt and yellow tie partly covered by his cardigan and anorak was telling Jackie that they had arrived at 4.00am to check in for their 6.00 o'clock flight to be told that the flight and their holiday had been cancelled.

Joe chipped in on the earpiece. "Wind him up, get him to lose his temper Phil get the whole group together, make it look like a wrinkly riot". Jackie and Phil knew the voice and where their bread was buttered and in no time at all there was a full-blown rumpus taking place.

A stern looking security official arrived, he had instructions to disperse the group and restore peace, but this would not happen when you are dealing with a group of war babies.

Gladys, a well built no messing about Black Country girl all of eighty years took careful aim at the official with her well laden cabin size hand bag, took a good swing and caught him smack where it really hurts flooring him with her one well aimed blow. A further official arrived to be met by Alfred who was to enjoy his ninetieth birthday come what may and pulled his warm fold up umbrella from its holster in his right trouser pocket to use it for what it was designed for and greeted him with a near fatal blow. The airport police were soon on hand and Phil filed a set of fabulous scenes of old ladies and gentlemen all screaming as they were arrested by the Police, bustled into security vans and taken with blue lights flashing, off into custody

"Great" said Joe "a real piece of live television."

The story made the top slot on breakfast TV throughout the UK with wrinkly riot stories and assault by police on senior citizens. They all spent the night in a hotel as there was not room in the cells. The next morning after a hearty breakfast they came up in front of the Magistrates. To deal with the case the court sat early to avoid disrupting the day's list and forty potential holiday makers packed into the number one court room.

By now the story had spread and every space was packed with reporters and public coming to get a view. The legal adviser stood and called for all to be upstanding a request which with the general hub-bub was ignored; at this point the three magistrates entered. The Chairman stood and surveyed the scene and banged her gavel to no avail, she was an impressive lady used to handing out severe reprimands and prison sentences. As she peered over her glasses that were perilously perched on the end of her nose she again banged her gavel and at the same time her glasses slipped from her nose and landed on the floor behind the legal adviser. At this point she finally gained control and the legal adviser swung round in his chair and stood to advise the chairman, the crushing noise of a pair of spectacles could be heard throughout the now silent court. The prosecution solicitor stood and outlined the case and recommended that they all be given 12 month orders not to breach the peace and that the charges of assault on police officers be dropped.

At this point the defence barrister rose to his feet. He happened to be defending in the Crown Court but the case had been adjourned. "Madame Chairman" he pushed out his chest in the way barristers have a habit of doing and his wig slipped to a slightly jaunty angle, the defence solicitor had briefed him and he was up for some fun with a no fee case. "Madame Chairman, you are looking here at forty beloved grannies and grandpas none of them has a single blemish on their characters. They have as much as eighty years as innocent citizens of Wednesfield, some have served their country and all have given years of voluntary service to the community. They set off at midnight yesterday to enjoy a holiday in the winter sun, at four o'clock in the morning they arrive to be confronted by burley security officers to be told that the holiday they had paid for from their hard earned savings without a by your leave was cancelled. Stranded at Birmingham Airport in their summer shirts and carrying their luggage would you not have sympathy for such a disappointed group? But what happened? They were set on by the security staff and airport police and manhandled into busses to be charged with some offence. Have we no more sympathy for this poor disillusioned group than to put them through a night of worry and anxiety before appearing before you today?" The two security officers rubbed their injured parts and shook their heads in disbelief. "Madame Chairman, the prosecution are calling for an order to prevent any further breach of the peace I ask the members of the bench to consider who it was that breached the peace, certainly not my innocent clients and to consider the gravity of the alleged offence and that they have all pleaded not guilty and would not on that basis accept an order that left them with any stain on their characters. Madam Chairman, if these were your grandparents before you would you consider that anything you have heard would make you, at worst give an absolute discharge or simply return a not guilty verdict." The chairman picked up her crushed glasses and together with her fellow magistrates retired.

Usually when magistrates retire they take the opportunity to have their first coffee before what looks to be a long day. Today they chose to almost immediately return to the court room.

The chairman struggled with her crumpled glasses and glared at the legal adviser, he was a little surprised as he had expected to be called in for the magistrates' deliberations, he was also looking forward to his first morning coffee.

Making her pronouncement the chairman looked out at the line of now slightly contrite senior citizens and tried with some difficulty to focus. "You are all victims in this case, by now you should be enjoying the mild winter of Menorca, the situation you found yourselves in was in no way your fault and I commend the restraint you showed with over enthusiastic security staff that were young enough to be your sons or even grandchildren so I am therefore dismissing this case and find you all innocent of any charges."

At this stage the court erupted and the magistrates raced to the retiring room for their cup of coffee.

As they left court Jackie and Phil were first in line for interviews as grannies and grandpas confessed to having more fun than they can remember and they had all been invited to spend their holiday in a place called Palma Nova in Majorca where they could continue their fun. But this time they were flying from East Midlands Airport, just as well thought Jackie.
"Get back to London and stir up their MP it's time the lazy bugger did something". So a shocked member for Wednesfield suddenly found himself dragged from obscurity to defend the rights of his constituents.

Sir Arthur Richards MP who had held his safe seat for 30 years and never once had to stand up and be accounted for, posed on the lawn opposite the Palace of Westminster. He promised to ask a question at Prime Minister's Question Time. Joe had known Sir Arthur when he was a reporter and the member was a new visionary who promised new hope to the run down area. After 30 years of obscurity and voting in the right place he had been lifted from obscurity and rewarded with a knighthood and then put back on the shelf.

Jackie was ready to go to war.

"Push him" said Joe. Jackie turned on her innocent look and he was lost. "With hundreds of holiday makers losing their hard earned vacations do you not consider that you should take a more positive approach than just ask a question?" pressed Jackie. Sir Arthur squirmed unaccustomed to being the centre of attention. "Well I need to go through the proper channels."

"Which channels do you propose to follow?" "Well errr." "Are you proposing to talk to the airline?" Sir Arthur grabbed at the lifeline. "Yes I intend to call them straight after this interview." "Are you intending to talk to their London office?" "Of course" he responded. "Did you not hear that their London office is closed?" He realised the trap had closed on him and the interview was over.

That could have been the end of the story except the computer started to whirr, newshounds were picking up similar stories throughout the UK, the story then broke in Sweden as the Royal Swedish naturist community found their holidays were cancelled, the final crunch came when The German Society for the Occupation of Deck Chairs found their holidays cancelled.

Jackie and Phil headed for the now closed London office of Menorca Airlines to find the offices now manned by an ever more aggressive security officer heading off a posse of geriatric protesters.

Vista Airlines were the largest airline flying to the island and also had an interest in the ferry service to the Spanish mainland. All had been suspended, San Christobal Holidays the main operator to Menorca had cancelled all holidays and all telecommunications had been cut.

"What the f**k is going on" shouted Joe, "who have we got on the island?"

"No one" came the response. "I want a team out there now I don't care how and the first newshound to report back will get a £10,000 bonus"

The race was on.

Chapter 3
Radley Airfield

R adley Airfield is an ex RAF base in the heart of Herefordshire and in January it is bloody cold reported newshound Jack. He had turned out for a residents' demonstration, these were usually good tea time viewing and were excellent for some rating points and on a quiet news day they could even go national. "Herefordshire residents are good for a protest, they get really excited, it must be living next to the Welsh, that's enough to get anybody going."

Slowly the bedraggled bunch of protestors arrived at the gate and Jack moved in for vox pops of the group and to get shots of their banners.

Border Surplus Military Vehicles had stock piled a massive range of every type of equipment from Land Rovers to trucks and track layers, all were parked on the runway like an army waiting to go to war. The Council had refused planning permission for the storage. BSMV had gone to appeal the decision and lost so the Council were now undertaking legal enforcement action to clear the site.

Border Surplus Military Vehicles was one of the many companies in a complex web of businesses owned by William Walkman-Roberts (with a hyphen). Jack had tracked down his chequered history thinking he may do an exposé on him when the time was right.

Bill Roberts had emerged as a snotty little kid from a council house in a Birmingham suburb. He had only one special quality that he could convince anyone of anything and was a natural salesman always just on the right side of a dodgy deal.

He left school at 15 without any qualifications, but like many boys that came out of the old Secondary Modern Boys School system he had a determination to be his own boss, working for someone else was never going to suit Bill.

His first venture was selling bibles door to door, he had seen a gap in the market for expensive family bibles and with his sweet angelic face would persuade the local Catholic Priest to give him a list of his parishioners on the pretext that he was taking the word to the heart of the family. He would then systematically work through the list on the basis that he was calling on behalf of the church and would sign up members to a monthly purchase payment for their elaborate but expensive bible.

Bill would close as many deals as possible before the word got out that the offer was a rip off and he would move on to the next innocent community. When he ran out of Catholics he tried the Church of England but for some reason, as he would say the C of Es never had the same conviction so this was a failure.

By now with a small first fortune, made with the help and guidance of God he disappeared off the scene to re-emerge as William Walkman-Roberts (with a hyphen). He had thought of changing his name to Calthorpe but discovered someone had got there before him. He also had a new posh accent and a misty history of never being quite straight about which minor public school he had gone to and which University had awarded him a degree in History.

He had seen an advertisement for the sale of residential freeholds. At the time they were low yield unpopular investments and all with about 25 years to run before the leasehold would revert to the freeholder.

William Walkman-Roberts (with a hyphen) was on a charge and picked up the investments for a song and could now claim that he owned large estates in areas as far apart as Northamptonshire and Kent, the next step was to use his expertise as a door to door salesman.

William Walkman-Roberts (with a hyphen) now Chairman of Walkman estates set about writing to every leaseholder warning them of the impending loss of their homes and how they should secure their investment for the future not just for them but for the future of their wives, children and grandchildren.

The offer valued each one at four times the price he paid and was for a limited period only.

In no time at all he had sold a quarter of all the investment and could sit back with a substantial income for a zero outlay, leasehold reform changed much of the long term benefit but William Walkman-Roberts (with a hyphen) was now on his way to amassing his second fortune this time from property.

Like most self made men he could never miss out on a deal and so he always felt the need to dabble in anything that could make a fast buck, hence Border Surplus Military Vehicles.

The Council officials were there in force to deliver the final papers and joining in the action were the local residents association who saw the Military hardware as a dangerous eye-saw and had mounted a local campaign to get the site cleared.

"Truck off," read one banner. "Make Love Not War" another, then "Hands off our Green Space" but "God is Love" seemed a bit out of place.

Jack gathered the angry group together and they climbed into a mini bus to go out to the site.

Lots of good material as they travelled around the airfield, Jack felt satisfied that the best was still to come.

Consternation as they arrived at the BSMV site. No Land Rovers, no trucks, no cranes, no track layers, hundreds of units all gone nothing left but a few patches of oil, the whole lot had disappeared.

No one had seen any movements, the entire fleet had disappeared. William Walkman-Roberts (with a hyphen) proprietor of BSMV was sitting waiting in his new Bentley. The Council officials waved, got back in their car and sped off, the protesters wanted blood but now they were not sure who's.

Jack pushed his way forward to the Bentley, William Walkman-Roberts (with a hyphen) puffed on his cigar blowing the smoke through the open window. "Where have they all gone?" pressed Jack. "I sold them." "I can see that but where have they all gone?" However hard he pushed Walkman-Roberts stonewalled.

A disappointed Jack looked at a story lost, but then let his mind wander like a true newshound.

How can you lose a complete convoy in a week?

He called the London desk and put out an all newshounds alert, who had bought it and where had they shipped it?

The hunt was on for a missing army.

Reports started to come back of a convoy of military vehicles passing through villages. At one stage thinking it was an army operation the police gave it an escort.

A young cub reporter from the local free sheet had emerged from the thatched sleepy village pub to be confronted by a thundering mass of an army on the move. He rubbed his eyes in disbelief and thought back to how many pints he had drunk, shook his head and started to transmit his story. On Joe's instructions any story that linked to the movement was important and he was to be called on any report.

The reports that were coming in were showing that the convoy had headed to Portsmouth and had loaded onto a roll-on-roll-off ferry. Jack raced to catch up but the ship had sailed three days earlier, he checked the ship's name and registration. All was correct the ship Empress of Cadiz had Spanish registration and all seemed in order.

As the ship passed through the straits of Gibraltar the news came through from Lloyds that the ship had changed hands at sea and was now registered to a Panamanian company and renamed "Bronze Butterfly"

Where in the Mediterranean was a ship with a cargo large enough to equip a small army heading?

Slowly the European community were starting to wake up. The computer whirred and the link was made.

"What the f**k is going on?" Joe was now on twenty four hour call.

Chapter 4
Down at the Stock Exchange

"Where is the stupid ars**le at the Stock Exchange?" Joe hated money men and all their paraphernalia Bulls, Stags and Bears be buggered all he wanted to know was what his stock was doing.

"Ok Henry what are all the clever sods doing?"

Henry was a retired stockbroker who had decided to be a newshound just for fun and that really aggravated Joe who thought that nothing was done just for fun.

"Making money on your stock," came the reply. "Up ten points in the last half hour, so you are even richer."

"And what's happening to airline shares?"

"All depressed except Global. They, as you know, had till midnight to raise the funds to save them from bankruptcy and a mystery buyer has stepped in and posted a multi million pound bond with the CAA and are to negotiate a deal with the potential liquidators. It's expected to complete a deal before the end of the day on the basis of it being a going concern. "And who is behind the deal?" barked Joe. "An unknown business group called Zebo International based in Panama, the office is just a name on the wall, the City is buzzing with rumours about who is behind the company but no news so far, but someone will have to put his head above the parapet soon or the CAA will make trouble." "And what's going on with hotels and property?" "Cristobal Holidays have sold all their interests in Menorca; they were the largest hotel and villa operator on the Island"

"Go on, now tell me about shipping." "Hey, how do you know all this? Lloyds have announced that Virgo Shipping has sold a fleet of 50 oil tankers a roll-on-roll-off freighter and five Menorcan ferries to an unknown ..." "Don't tell me, an unknown group of businessmen" "How do you know all this?" "Never mind how just keep me posted." Joe pulled the plug.

"Circulate all this to Newshounds Worldwide I want to know where all this money is coming from and who is behind it." Joe's nose twitched, he smelt a rat. Somehow this is all linked. How could an international airline, a major shipping company and a significant holiday company sale be linked? He leant back in his red leather swivel chair and called for a coffee and started to piece the bits together and look for a connection.

Chapter 5
Butterfly World

"What's a Bronze F***ing Butterfly got to do with this lot?" "It keeps coming back in our reports" said the now petrified young news editor. "Then find out what it is you daft bugger." Joe was warming up for the day. "I've sent Cedric the pansy down to the World Butterfly centre at Witney, he knows all about flowers and trees, do you remember he did that piece on the sex life of a one legged toad -- One skip and a hump." "I can't wait, let me know when the story is coming in" snorted Joe.

Cedric was a timid man, it wasn't that he didn't like people he just didn't know how to talk to them, he could talk for hours to a grasshopper and he found beetles quite entertaining, robins never stood still long enough to really communicate, but his great joy were goldfish.

Goldfish he felt could really relate to him as however boring he felt he may have been the goldfish would never remember so he could repeat the same story over and over again as the poor fish went on its never ending circular journey.

Cedric had never been asked to do anything before and his scientific study of the mating habits of a one legged toad had for some reason been a world wide hit, this continued to provide him with enough in repeat fees to pay for all his other research that never seemed to get screened.

As he arrived at the World Butterfly Centre he carefully parked his immaculate, three speed Sturmey Archer, Classic Raleigh Superb 1956 one careful owner bicycle, complete with the all encasing chain guard and polished pedals, not to forget the battery pack encased on the back frame upright and the crowning glory of a

Lucas tail light shaped like a tube with a red knob on the end. Proudly shining out through the dark nights was the chrome plated lamp that had a little pointer switch to turn it to dip and avoid glaring in the eyes of on coming motorists. This was connected to the circular generator on the front wheel. All this was finished in a dark green paint and with gold coloured pencil lines to highlight the greatness of the British Cycle manufacturing industry. Cedric if anything was a stickler for detail, he carefully chained his bike to the railings, re set the combination lock writing down the number on a piece of two inch by one inch card that he folded and pushed inside the small hole in the end of the rubber hand grips at the end of the handlebars, he then placed a second copy in the pocket of his corduroy trousers feeling confident that if he lost his trousers he would still have a copy of the combination in his handlebars.

As a last final security he locked the handlebars using the distinctive Raleigh lock set in the top of the front forks.

He checked the H. Samuel Everight watch that his father had left him, it was precisely 3.00 o'clock as he entered the great glass dome that was the World Butterfly Centre. Professor Wallace stood waiting for him.

Professor Wallace was a tall but rather crumpled man with grey hair and a beard that had exploded to give him a God like look, his hair had strands of coloured dye making it look like a rainbow and he wore a shirt and trousers to match making him look like some weird tropical plant.

As Cedric got closer he could see that intertwined with his hair was a mass of every type of butterfly you could imagine. The news editor called Joe. "You must see this." "Oh f***ing hell somebody break his leg and film them shagging and we can use it on a late night spot."

The Professor probably had a deep strong voice but all you could hear was a soft gentle singing murmur as he spoke to the butterflies. Here was Cedric's soul mate.

As he stretched out his massive hand the butterflies rose as if on a signal and circled away into the high tropical dome of the glass pavilion. Cedric put out his hand to shake and as he did so a small white butterfly settled on his index finger.

"You have a friend." Cedric had a great urge to talk to the insect but was overcome by the Professor's presence. "She likes you." A feeling of joy came over him and he felt that he had come home, he and the Professor needed no words they just understood each other.

"For Christ's sake say something" barked Joe. The spell was broken Cedric was here to do a job. "Hello" said Cedric. "Please call me Archibald or Archie for short. What can I do for you?" "I came to ask you about the Bronze Butterfly" he said timidly. "Follow me" and off they went with Archie in full flood.

"Keep him in camera - just think of him as the one legged toad" "Don't let it near your Pelargoniums or your Geraniums the little devil will do for the lot, first came here in a shipment of pot plants but couldn't cope with the cold, likes it nice and warm. Beautiful little creature both sexes look the same." A brown butterfly landed on Archie's hand, Cedric peered very close and at the same time the third eye gave the monitor a perfect view.

"They're clever little things they grow long tails with big eye spots that will see off any predator. Of course they are a pest and not protected anywhere, they arrived in the Balearic Islands in 1987 and have since spread to mainland Spain, France, Italy and even as far as Malta." "Ask the bugger where they came from."

"And where did they come from Archie?"
"Oh they're big in South Africa."
"Bingo" shouted Joe in a voice that nearly blew the ear piece off, the entire collection of butterflies and they soared into the roof and the studio pulled the plug.

Chapter 6
The Last Ferry

Alfonso worked the Barcelona centre as a newshound and was the first to respond to Joe's call to get on the island; he raced to the port on his scooter to find the whole area in chaos. Four of the island ferries had docked, their cars and passengers disembarked and the last, MS Pride of Menorca 5 was lined up to come alongside.

Alfonso pushed to get to the front of the throng. "Why are all the ferries here at once? They should be running a two hourly service." The harbour official saw nothing unusual. "It's the winter timetable; everyone wants to get off for a holiday before the season starts." Slowly the roll-on-roll-off ferry came to the jetty and raised her bow to let the hundred plus vehicles disembark, all were packed solid with everything you could imagine from furniture to beds strapped to the car roofs. He tried to speak to passengers as they came off but they all remained silent not one would speak to him.

He raced to the ticket office only to be told that the boat was full and not even one foot passenger ticket was available. He waited until the ship was empty and the waiting cars and passengers started to check in only to see all the ship's crew disembark. Perhaps that was not unusual as crews needed to change at some time, but as he got closer he saw the new officers and crew had different uniforms and had a badge that looked like a butterfly.

Joe watched as the Spanish newshound made his way towards the ticket gate as he got to the barrier the officer was distracted and he managed to slip aboard.

"Don't run that piece." screamed Joe, but it was too late it was already out across the

Iberian Peninsula and without knowing Alfonso was now a hunted man.

It was soon obvious to him that none of the passengers were Spanish or for that matter English, they all spoke with an accent that was strange to him, he felt the best thing to do was keep quiet and watch and listen he also had the sense to keep broadcasting but by now Joe had stopped transmitting.

The two hour journey was passing rapidly and as they approached the Island he could see a large ship moving into Mahon harbour, the name on the stern was very clear "The Bronze Butterfly"

As they passed between the first fairway marker buoys that flashed their red and green signals Alfonso began to pick out lines of white motor yachts, the sort you would only see in such number in Monte Carlo for the Grand Prix, each one with one, two or even three helicopter landing pads with its own helicopter. Mounted on the after deck of each craft was a massive missile launcher, and fluttering from the jack staff of each one was an ensign of green with what looked like a yellow image that Alfonso could not make out. "Shit" exclaimed Joe. "They've got a bigger f*****g navy than ours." It was no surprise as the roll-on-roll-off cargo ship raised its bow and an army of newly painted military vehicles each clearly showing a Bronze Butterfly on a green square started to emerge on to the shore. "And it looks like they have got half of our army as well" offered the news editor.

The officers on the ferry had clearly had a warning of an intruder and suddenly transmission ended and the sound went dead.

Joe was at his best. "Warn all stations, just send edited highlights and don't give the whole game away, we can then run the full story to catch both breakfast and evening transmissions worldwide and maximise the rating points."

"What about Alfonso?"

"What do you mean what about Alfonso, he's going to be rich he's hit pay dirt."

The news editor's comment that he could be both rich and dead got lost in the excitement.

Amongst all the excitement an urgent call came through from the Stock Exchange. All three detailed acquisitions were now trading as "The Bronze Butterfly." The Stock Exchange was in turmoil.

Chapter 7
The First Landing

J ackie and Phil were quick off the mark. Stansted offered the best option for an instant booking on a cheap flight to Majorca. With just their hand luggage they were able to avoid the lines of shuffling, canvas shoed grandparents off to find a warmer winter in Tenerife, Ibiza or even further afield.

"They all look the same" commented Phil. All the ladies with shiny velour track suits and trainers ready to make the dash for the window seat with the most leg room and the men with stretch top trousers, anoraks and easy fit Velcro tab shoes trying to convince their wives that the bag stuffed with everything including the teapot and tea bags won't fit into the size guide to allow it as hand luggage. Blue rinse, white flat caps and the smell of mothballs filled the air with that special aroma of grandparents.

All around were groups of people eating their last meal in England of ham sandwiches before they embarked on this year's adventure. Jackie and Phil had got a last minute booking on the 7.35am flight to Majorca. They had reckoned that the best shot they had was to persuade a fisherman under the cover of darkness to take them as near as possible to a Menorcan beach and then make the short trip ashore by dinghy.

Getting through the airport security with their cameras and sound equipment was always a problem and they had the inevitable strip search but after giving proof that they were who they said they were the tired officers let them go on to passport control.

No sooner were they through and the announcement of their flight was called and a sea of white caps and blue rinses rose like a tidal wave to the departure pier and yet more checks before they clumped down the walkway to crush onto the flight. Hand luggage was strewn all over the aisle and oversize bags were pushed into lockers. Ultimately they all settled down and Jackie and Phil finally boarded like royalty to take up two seats either side of the aisle ready to sleep through the 2 ¼ hour journey to who knew what.

The lady next to Phil wanted to talk and show him pictures of her grandchildren even before takeoff. He recovered his seat belt from beneath her large bottom and secured it; he vaguely remembered the hostess checking him over and fell into a deep sleep before the end of the safety check.

Phil felt the change in the engine note as the plane began its long descent to its destination and as he woke he realised that the woman next to him was still talking and showing him pictures. She's in training for the long hours in the hotel lounge competing with all the other grannies for the most boring family, he thought. He could hear her saying to him "how nice it's been to travel with such an interesting person who is such a good listener, my husband always goes to sleep." He sympathised with her just as her husband woke with an urgent need for the toilet, at this moment a hundred other husbands woke with the same need and chaos broke out.

As only a fraction would get to the toilet before the plane landed Phil thanked modern science for incontinence pads.

Jackie had fared no better, she had been wading through her book, the one luxury she allowed herself on these jaunts. It was an account of the first five years of the Cameron coalition and a detailed account of how they had beaten the recession.

Sitting next to her was a man with ginger dyed hair who had clearly not been to bed all night and wanted to make up for the loss, as he slipped down the seat his head dropped to one side and rested on Jackie's shoulder; however much she wriggled it was there for the duration.

She tried to read and was just getting into the details of a confidential Cabinet meeting and a discussion between David Cameron and George Osborne when the snoring started, strangely it seemed to fit quite well as she visualised one of the older Cabinet members catching forty winks.

The pilot put the plane down quite heavily to counter a strong cross wind. A draft of moth balls momentarily countered the air conditioning, false teeth clicked firmly together and the wrinkly army were on the move.

Passing through the baggage hall was easy as Jackie and Phil had only hand luggage so they were soon out of the airport and into a taxi heading north to Puerto Pollensa. They had chosen this location from a holiday brochure that gave views of its harbour with fishing boats so they reckoned that would be their best shot.

The taxi dropped them at the harbour and while Phil set off to negotiate with a fisherman Jackie went to sort out a rubber dinghy, this proved harder than she had thought as there is only a limited market for rubber dinghies with even the active senior citizens at this time of the year.

All the shops seemed to have sold out and were waiting for their spring stock, after a long trawl she found an inflatable semi rigid canoe that would serve their purpose quite well.

After a struggle she managed to get it to their meeting point which was the only Spanish restaurant on the quay, all the others looked to be offering Bratwurst and

Chips or a real English breakfast together with as much beer as you can drink.

Phil had already arrived and was ordering a full English Breakfast from surprisingly the English proprietor. Looking at the short choppy Mediterranean sea beyond the harbour Jackie decided to do the same working on the basis that she didn't know where her next meal would come from or if she would hold this one down once they were at sea. News takes a long time to travel in Spain and no one had picked up the details of what had happened on an island just across the water. The interest ranged from "I don't care I'm on holiday" to "ignore it and it will go away" as the new arrivals with today's papers were busy telling everyone what they knew.

The fisherman had doubted the reasons for why they had wanted to do a night trip to Menorca. This is where my wife and I fell in love and consummated our passion was the best Phil could come up with and it did well enough along with a week's money for one night's work so the deal was done.

Jackie and Phil checked into a small hotel and paid in advance for one day, even in these modern times the desk receptionist looked suspicious but it was cash so why should she worry.

Whenever they had time to kill they usually spent it the same way, turn off their cameras climb into bed together make passionate love, fall asleep and wake up fresh for their next job. This time they forgot to switch off and gave the newsroom some great late night footage.

It was just getting dark as they made their way to the harbour carrying their collapsible canoe and a few provisions. They found the boat with skipper and another hand ready waiting for them; they quickly loaded the cargo and slipped the mooring. The little ship's lights reflected in the calm water of the harbour; nothing stirred as they made progress towards the flashing red and green markers that identified the entrance, all was going well apart from the smell of dead fish that came from the hold and the feeling that the boat was covered in the scales of fish from earlier trips.

Once through the harbour entrance the sea began to live up to the expectations of a January night in the Med with that short uncomfortable wave motion that sets up the traditional roll of a fishing boat used to spending hours at sea. As they rounded Cap de Formentor they lost the protection of the lee shore and began to feel the full impact of a force 6 westerly. The fishing boat now took on a heavier rolling motion as she beamed both wind and sea on the port side, the engine also changed note as it drove the propeller through the waves, the bow was now burying itself into each roller and the stern would come out of the water to let out a belch of diesel fumes. Jackie took over the wheel and with each movement looked happier and happier. The fishermen could not take their eyes off the body that moved to every movement the craft made for her. This was the moment dreams were made of.

For Phil life was less happy he had now fallen in love with a bucket and clasping it close to his chest thought only of life after death.

The night wore on with Jackie at the wheel and Phil at the bucket. The distant coastline of Menorca came into view on the rare occasions when the moon broke through the cloud and then some lights could be seen ashore.

The wind eased and came round to the south setting up a change in the motion, it was time to get the canoe ready, Phil rallied and gave up the bucket.

Suddenly as if from nowhere they heard the unmistakable throb of big twin turbo diesels and they saw in the dawn light a large white ship that looked like a luxury yacht. The skipper quickly cut the speed and proceeded to get his nets over the side while on the other side Jackie and Phil boarded their canoe and paddled silently for the shore.

They could see in the distance the yacht coming alongside the small fishing boat. The vessel was massive and in the silhouette they could see it was bristling with an armoury extensive enough to meet any incident. The only lights showing were the glow of instruments lighting up the face of the bearded captain; as the ship manoeuvred they saw not one but two helicopters on the afterdeck. Suddenly a blaze of light shone down onto the little boat blinding all on board and a loud hailer pierced the early morning sounds. "This is a restricted area what are you doing here?" barked out a faceless voice. "Fishing" came the reply. "Well get the hell out of here now" and being satisfied that all was in order escorted them away from the Menorca coast. As the yacht turned to head away from the coast Phil and Jackie clearly saw a helicopter ready for takeoff with an armed crew on board and the outline of a large gun ready and manned on the after deck and the Bronze Butterfly flag flying from the jack staff.

"That could have been for us" they thought and the fact that this was not some fun game but a serious life and death escapade came crashing into their minds and despite the cold of the morning they began to sweat. First step over.

Back in the studio Joe had sat up all night and revelled in such super television.

Chapter 8
A Town at War

The proposed landfall was to be Son Bou as Jackie had spent a holiday here and could remember the layout, in fact the wind had taken them further down the coast and they discovered they were on the beach at Santo Tomas.

Dawn was now breaking and they needed to escape inland their only option was to steal a car, the hotel car park was full and had security cameras so they opted to walk to the line of shops and found a convenient Seat parked complete with keys and a half full tank of diesel.

They set off along the narrow lane that took them to the main East West Highway that runs from the capital Mahon in the east to Ciudadela in the west.

As they came to the junction the traffic was solid but most of all it was convoys of military vehicles of every sort all travelling east. There was always a danger that speech could be picked up locally but Jackie broke radio silence back to the studio. "What the hell is going on? This is a war zone." Joe broke in "we don't know yet but keep your heads down and stay silent. By the way great un- coverage you gave us yesterday I never knew about the tattoo." At that point Joe switched off but Jackie still heard the newsroom erupt in shouts and wolf whistles. "Bastards."

Phil turned right onto the highway and headed towards Mahon. The traffic was much lighter in this direction and they made good progress. Up in front of them they could see what looked like a road block so they decided to stop, dig into their provisions and take stock, so they pulled over just before the junction that would take them into the road to Alaior and concealed their car on a small track.

They both went into the bushes to do what people have to do and came out to be confronted by a group of horsemen all dressed from head to foot in black and mounted on pure bred massive Spanish horses. Without a word being spoken they were both lifted onto the back of a horse behind a rider and were soon galloping off up the mountainside towards Alaior.

For Jackie the experience was wonderful and as they raced through the trees holding on to her mystery captor she sang one of her favourite songs "Off with the raggle taggle Gypsies." For Phil it was a different experience he felt that his testicles were being crushed and wished he was back watching horses from the Champagne Bar at Ascot.

The market square at Alaior is fed by a network of cobbled streets and as they rode in the clatter of the hooves of even more horses filled the air with a mediaeval sound that intensified the excitement of this ancient town.

Jackie remembered she had been here before and seen the horse race that left onlookers pinned into doorways as riders and horses cantered through the centre lashing out with whips onto both horses and riders as everything went faster and faster.

Jackie let go of the rider as they came to a halt, he swung his leg over the horses head and all in a single action plucked her from the horse to bring her gently back to her feet.

Joe back in the studio was captivated; he desperately wanted to give her instructions but didn't dare break her cover, "if only I could run this now".

As they spoke three edited versions were ready to role, the short, medium and long. The first of the morning sun broke through into the village, the perspiration of both men and horses filled the square like a low cloud. At the far end was a giant of a man seated on a pure white stallion, he rode forward until his horse almost stood on Jackie's toes but instead stepped over her feet and left its master free to slide from its back to stand almost touching her but not so close as to intimidate. "Welcome Jackie," he said in a soft tone with only the slightest of an accent. "We have been waiting for you. I am Ferrario the leader of my people on Menorca.

She felt her legs going weak at the sight of this beautiful man. Unlike any Spaniard she had ever seen he had dark wavy hair going silver at the sides with greying eyebrows, soft blue eyes and a gentle but well worn bronzed face with a tall muscular frame.

"Run it all" shouted Joe and a cheer went up around the newsroom as they all counted their bonuses.

"What about Jackie and Phil" pleaded the young assistant news editor. Joe scowled "are you sure you're in the right job?" and at that moment he was pretty sure he wasn't.

The spell was broken as Phil stepped forward and demanded to know how he knew of their movements.

"I have followed you ever since you left England every move you made was monitored, I have a private satellite feed that tracked your cameras and of course I have many friends in high places. I went to school at Eton and Oxford." He then raised his hand to indicate that he would not answer any more questions.

"Now my dear is there anything that is in my power to give you that you would like?" Without thinking twice. "Something to eat and drink." Jackie realised that she had not had a meal since previous day and all that Phil had had was in the bucket.

Ferrario waved the way to a café in the square and took them inside, awaiting them was a readymade spread of all the delights that Menorca had to offer, was there anything she wanted that he had not arranged. Every sort of Tapas dish in every recipe book you had ever seen was spread across the white table cloth together with a range of chilled fresh drinks.

They made rapid work of lightening the table and sat back in their chairs waiting for the next move. "Where do we go from here?" asked Phil. "We want you to be our Ambassadors to the Bronze Butterfly State. Let me tell you something about us, our history and what is happening on our Island. Throughout the centuries our land has been occupied by many different countries going back to the Greeks, Romans, Phoenicians, French even the English and more recently the Italians, you could also say the Spanish and now the Bronze Butterfly.

"As mountain people we have lived uninterrupted for over 2,000 years, we are the true Menorcans and are a race apart from Spain and the mainland.

"We have our own culture, live off the land and are self sufficient, what we trade pays for all our external needs and we are happy to have been left alone in this modern high speed world.

"Conquerors over the centuries have only wanted the great Mediterranean ports at Mahon and Ciudadela and more recently the Airport and the sandy holiday beaches. We have no desire for any of these. We seek a peaceful co-existence with whoever lives on this island and that is what we want you to tell the world."

Little did they know but the world was either waking up or going to bed with that news now.

Also the male population were waiting for the 9.00pm watershed to see the eagerly billed see Jackie and Phil get closer than ever in our uncensored un-coverage. Joe wanted to add "It beats one legged shagging toads." On this occasion he got talked out of it.

Chapter 9
First Confrontation

With the intimate details of the Menorcan adventure now on every television screen the pressure was on for an early meeting. Contact was being made between the leaders of both sides and arrangements made for a car with escort to collect Jackie and Phil that evening. Everyone was now crowding around the television in the café as the short, medium and long versions were running.

"And now live coverage of the scenes in Alaior at the heart of the Mediterranean Island of Menorca, Europe" (for the benefit of the American viewer) stated the link man as only link men selling a story can. These were interspersed with world comment.

Admiral Sir Jack Anstruther Featherstonehaugh retired stated the obvious. "There is enough firepower there to blow half the world in two." "We need to consider all the facts to allow us to make a reasoned comment and we will take it to our first available emergency meeting next month" was the view of the EU President. NATO wanted to know who they were so they could decide which side to be on. Great Britain offered to negotiate a settlement. The Italians backed both sides. The Lepidopterist Freedom Movement claimed responsibility. Russia and China were still in bed.

The US Mediterranean fleet was mobilised and the entire world watched television and up went the rating points as did the shares in Third Eye News, while Joe Dyke rubbed his hands with glee. Arrangements were made for a meeting in Mahon and a car would collect them at 8.00pm that evening.

"Couldn't be better" shouted Joe "perfect timing we will hit pay dirt world wide"

"Now we have time to spare" said Ferrario turning to Jackie "time to sing for your supper." With the thought of a worldwide audience Jackie didn't need to think about it twice. She looked for the mike and the Karaoke but from nowhere a guitarist appeared and the performance of Jackie's life began. Cole Porter, Gershwin, Ellington, Lloyd-Webber she took the impromptu audience by storm from tears to laughter even to a sing along, her range went from Piaff to Fitzgerald, Holiday to Bassey, she gave them the works.

Soon the time came to depart, this time by a local car not on horseback, they gave their farewells and Ferrario thanked them with a reminder that he would be watching their every move.

Phil thought that if he ever saw a bed again he would never forget to turn the camera and sound off.

The car swerved and bumped as it went down the road to meet the main highway, here a large black car was waiting for them together with two motorcycle outriders. They travelled in silence all the way to the capital even Joe had nothing to say. Soon they came into the outskirts of the town and dropped down towards the harbour.

The provisional Government as they now described themselves had taken up residence in a large conference hotel with a grand entrance. They were met by uniformed guards and escorted to an impressive seminar room; in the centre was a large circular table.

As they walked in double doors at the other end of the room opened and a tall impressive man that looked like he had spent a lifetime out of doors entered. "I am Pieter Laurens" he said in a deep South

African accent. With him was a small entourage.

He then introduced the team. "This is Dieter Shenken, George Lea, Emeline Botichelli and Pierre Robberchou. You will see that we all have strong European names. We all have both South African and EU passports; amongst our followers we have every country in the EU represented and of course Alfonso here is one of your newshounds.

"Alfonso is co operating with us interpreting world news as it comes in and assessing the reaction. You see the Third Eye is no longer an impartial observer, you and your network of affiliate stations worldwide have now become a part of the action and the message you carry across the networks will play a major part in our future and the solution. Please sit down. Can we offer you tea or coffee?"

Phil and Jackie moved to the large round table. They had the distinct feeling that they were now just pawns in a game and no longer in control of their actions. Phil was the first to speak. "We are here to negotiate on behalf of the mountain residents." Pieter Laurens raised his large hand and stopped his speech. "We know why you are here, we have seen it all on television news but you have a more important role to play. We are not conquerors seeking to colonise and steal from the native population, we are here to take back what we have a right to and we are the legitimate owners of the vast majority of this island. Ferrario and his community have the right of ownership to their land and we respect and will live in peace with them, it is for them to live their lives as they wish without interference from us. Ferrario and his people will have full rights to participate in our interim Parliament and be free to participate in our actions as will any other residents that remain on the island. It is now for us to put forward our peaceful proposals to the world and let them be the judge of our actions."

Chapter 10
The Challenge

Everyone was now seated and all three newshounds were now transmitting getting first class angles from all positions round the table. Joe was transfixed. Never in his wildest dreams could he have believed that his news network could hold such a position, for once in his life he was speechless; he had even stopped watching the rating monitors, he needn't worry they were off the scale worldwide.

"Our plan is no secret, through your eyes the world is watching and waiting, what do we want, what are our motives, is the world heading to some new war?" Pieter Laurens settled back into a large comfortable leather chair, his great hands and gnarled face seemed to fit perfectly into the situation, he was commanding but gentle, almost the vision of everyone's great loved uncle. His voice was soft but powerful giving a feeling of absolute trust a man that would not harm a fly but no fly would dare take the chance. His blue eyes looked deep into each face around the table and at the same time looked into every home across the world; the three newshawk cameras were there to pick up every movement.

"The answer is simple, we have bought what many countries spend £millions to sell. The Greek Islands have no value beyond their tourism benefit; the Canaries again offer little more, the Balearics also fall into the same category. They are possessions that have no value beyond being a playground for the rest of Europe. What we bring is a massive investment. We are different from Gibraltar, we are not an outpost of some other state, you could say we read the holiday brochures, the property advertisements are very enticing, you have sold us on the climate and the island's beauty and we have bought what we saw.

"So here we are, but we are here to stay so what is the difference from what you have marketed to the world for the last fifty years?

"You have sold your soul and we have bought it, but not as a time share, a villa holiday, a two week holiday or a hen weekend but as a new living community independent of cash handouts.

"Our intention is to develop our free state as an independent tax free economic centre free of bureaucracy, our financial markets will complement those of the great world centres, our investments will regenerate the dying old world. As you can imagine what we have achieved has not been done by a group of Boars on the great trek north, but by financial and business magnets from all over the globe. At the heart of every country from Europe to America and

Africa to Asia there are supporters of our cause and investors that have helped to get us here. You will have seen that the island is now fortified with firepower enough to defend our home, the registration of the luxury yachts will give you an indication of our support.

"Our fortification on sea, land and in the air is not a threat it is a statement of our intent, the contribution we are able to make far exceeds the cost and who would wish to be the first nation to fire on its own nationals?

"Our forbears travelled the seas to bring great wealth to our mother countries; indeed much of the blood that was spilt in the name of nations is on your hands. Our people are not economic migrants from some far land we are your people coming home to take up our rightful possessions.

"My request to you is that we take our case to the United Nations and let them determine the future of our rainbow community." Peiter Laurens raised his hands with the palms facing upwards in a gesture of friendship and instantly all three cameras went dead.

Joe leant back in his chair. "So who will blink first?"

Chapter 11
World Reaction

Before the cameras had gone dead the Spanish fleet was moving into position with landing craft ready to launch, helicopters with troops waiting for instructions to commence the assault and missiles trained on key sites. As dawn broke it became obvious that there was a luxury yacht in every Menorcan bay and observers could see families with young children walking the sea front promenades, further data was coming back that each cliff top was armed and ready for action. Spain was ready to set about a long term blockade of the island. Worldwide public opinion was now getting fed back to the Bronze Butterfly media centre, none of the European states was prepared to be too hasty. With people sending good will messages to family and friends that were now on the island newshounds were besieged by calls to send their love to sons, daughters, grandchildren and friends. At the same time big business that had helped to finance the project were pressuring their governments to stand back from actions that could prove a disaster at the Polls for any forthcoming elections. What was happening was that the people were taking control of foreign policy and the pressure was on for a rapid solution before it got out of hand.

Every local broadcaster was running wall to wall coverage, the Pope was calling for peace, the lines between the world leaders were red hot. Everyone was calling for Spain to back off. How could they be persuaded? They now had the short straw and needed to save face with a negotiated settlement.

If they were to take an aggressive position they would need to blow a mass of luxury yachts out of the water and if they moved first how would they deal with an attack on private property in a premier holiday destination? Landing by helicopters held the same danger. The whole Spanish economy stood at risk depending on their action. Secret talks began between the major leaders. The first action was to pull back to a five mile distance and put the troops on to a state of standby, this took the heat out of the situation. The Spanish view was still to concede nothing, they were still smarting from the Basque and Catalonian separatist movements that were threatening the breakup of Spain and they were not in a mood to make any concessions.

To make comparisons with Gibraltar was like throwing petrol on the fire. The situation of the Channel Islands and the Isle of Man even Monaco did little to pacify a country that through no fault of its own was about to lose a possession. Confidential conversations continued to take place between leaders and the Spanish Government and in the meantime public opinion was boiling and calling for a settlement. Back in London Joe surveyed his empire,

"Every bloody Government says it wants to do what the people want, now for the first time they have got it in the face and they don't know what to do."

Chapter 12
European Union

All the EU countries now had a comprehensive list of the new residents of Menorca and sure enough of the several thousand families of men women and children every country had a significant number all holding EU and South African passports.

The governments were now realising that what they had was in many respects no different to what happened every year when their holiday makers went to effectively occupy all the Mediterranean islands and most of the coast as well. They also had many ex pats living in these areas so what was different, surely in Spain's case this was more or less what they had encouraged. A small minority regarded this attitude as a Chamberlain style of appeasement and were waiting for someone to fly back to Brussels with a note saying "peace in our time," but public opinion was siding with the families of the new settlers.

Every seat in the vast EU Parliament was occupied, the clerks, the press gallery and the interpreters all waiting for the great debate to commence.

The Chamber went silent as the President entered and took up his seat; there was no need to call the members to order you could have heard a pin drop.

"Who has been harmed" asked the EU President addressing the Parliament, "these are our people returning home from a long journey should we not now welcome them?"

The Parliament then broke into chaos with everyone wanting to speak with every language being shouted and trying to be heard.

At this point the President was unable to call the members to order and adjourned the debate until they returned from their break in three weeks time.

Chapter 13
The United Nations

Pieter stood at the podium and surveyed the members, not a sound could be heard. "Mr. Secretary General, brothers, sisters because that's what you are brothers and sisters bringing peace to this troubled world." The delegates sat back to listen, some in English and some with monotonous translations. Pieter Laurens had resolutely walked to the podium, he had requested and been granted an opportunity to address the great United Nations, his safety had been guaranteed and a private jet had taken him to Paris and then by scheduled flight to New York.

He now looked larger than life, his gnarled hands rested gently on the podium, his full beard and curly hair surrounding a bronzed wrinkled face and his deep set blue eyes surveyed the chamber making every member think that he was speaking only to them.

His deep baritone voice rang out in a clear South African accent that went to every corner, not a soul moved.

Jackie and Phil had travelled with him and now had key positions in front of the podium. Joe sat close to his monitor this was his story and he was going to milk it for all it was worth.

"Brothers, sisters where do we begin? How far back in the history of our nations should we delve, to China, Egypt, Ancient Greece indeed perhaps we should turn to Italy and the history of the Roman Empire or to more recent history. He turned to the Italian Ambassador and paused giving him a long piercing look. For some reason there was some discomfort in the delegation. Mr Ambassador does your country have some recent history in the Balearics, was it not in 1936 that Italy invaded Majorca and in a brutal occupation murdered 3,000 citizens?" He then went on and as he named each country he turned to look at their delegation "are you all free from guilt?" Jackie concentrated her eyes on every move he made and Phil made his mark on the response of each Ambassador. He turned to address Spain. "The record of that great country and its Conquistadors did not cover that noble state in South American glory. Looking to Great Britain those honourable Pilgrim Fathers bought a country for a handful of beads, won their independence and went on to take the rest of the land by theft. The British then went on to colonise South Africa, Australia, New Zealand, India indeed more than half the world all at the cost of their native populations.

"Indeed Great Britain itself has taken and occupied Menorca by force on two occasions.

More recently we see the takeover of Argentina by Italians. But where is this taking us? The world accepts the progressive movement of mass populations from the east moving west as the western Asian population takes up its right to relocate in peace. Almost every Member State here today has a history of rape, pillage, theft, slavery and murder, none of you is without blame.

"The Bronze Butterfly State has done none of these.

"Every year not just islands but whole regions sell themselves to the tourist masses, populations multiply many times over, what is different is that we are here to stay, not as expats but as true residents. Our skills in all ranges, business, science, agriculture the arts and medicine are as good as any in the world.

"Our offer to Europe and the world is a new powerhouse of creative thinking unfettered by the politics of State. We have now completed the purchase of the vast majority of properties, businesses and utilities; we own the airline, the ferry company, hotels and a bank. In fact the Bronze Butterfly State now owns the Island of Menorca. So who has lost out as a result of our actions, the population have been compensated not with beads but with the market price for their property and a lump sum to pay for their relocation, this is in no way different to what you are proposing to many of your immigrants to persuade them to return home.

"My people are citizens of the world. We have occupied the southern tip of Africa but the time has now come for us to return that state to its rightful occupants and for us to return home.

"In this strange topsy turvey world we live in who has the right of possession? Most of us are mongrels that came from thousands of years of moving populations; we all share in a common blood of history. Today we talk of taking down barriers and pretend that we have a universal brotherhood. Now is your chance to show that this is not idle talk but a real commitment."

The chamber erupted with a standing ovation. Every nation except Spain was on their feet, the people had spoken and no politician was going to stand in the way.

Chapter 14
Realisation

Back in Madrid the Cabinet watched in horror as the realisation came over them that they had lost the battle and now needed to work for a peaceful conclusion.

As they all shouted and argued their voices resonated high up to the ornate plasterwork and the magnificent ceiling of the Cabinet room. There, resting on the grand chandelier a butterfly exercised its wings, gently moving to show the large black eyes and the twin tails creating the menacing look that was exclusive to the Bronze Butterfly.

The end...... or just the beginning.